upbeat

Cultivating the right attitude to **thrive** in tough times.

rajesh setty

Published by
Ashoka Books
an imprint of Rvive Books

Published by Ashoka Books, an imprint of Rvive Books
Creative Management Partners, LLC
8 Gray's Farm Road, Weston, CT 06883
www.rvive.com

ISBN: 9781935073031
For bulk sales or custom publishing opportunities,
please contact the publisher.

Distributed by Ingram Publisher Services

Printed in Canada
First Printing: April 2009

10 9 8 7 6 5 4 3 2 1

Cover, Book design and composition by: Purplepatch
Services LLC (www.purplepatchservices.com)

Stay upbeat!
Warmly
Rajesh

upbeat

Cultivating the right attitude to **thrive** in tough times.

rajesh setty

To
My Teacher

Shri G.Seetharam

who showed me how easy it is to stay Upbeat
and I have not looked at life in any other way
since 1986!

Advance Praise

"Rajesh Setty's excellent book on starting and building companies during tough economic times is not simply another "how to" book of good practices. It actually improves how you fundamentally think about building your business, both during good and bad times."

Abe Kleinfeld
President and CEO, nCircle Network Security, Inc.

"Raj says, "Giving up is easy. Anyone can do it." He's almost right. It is easy, but you're not going to do it. This book outlines exactly why this is the very best moment to start something, to make an impact, to create a better world. Hurry. Start."

Seth Godin, author of *Tribes*

"In this timely, yet tender work, Setty offers important advice for business people from all walks. His message is simple: Manage your attitude and outlook. During these perilous times, that may be the most important thing that leaders can coach in their people."

Tim Sanders
Author of *Saving The World At Work* and
former Chief Solutions Officer at Yahoo!

Foreword by Russ Fradin

M any companies today are worried about how to survive, when their focus should be on how to thrive. I'm a strong believer that the one thing all successful companies have in common is that they know how to execute on their core business. After all, it is easy to become distracted. Some companies focus too much energy on internal issues—such as developing the perfect vision, dreaming up the most-brilliant brand campaign, or fine-tuning the organization structure. They forget to keep their customers' needs and priorities first.

Other companies, in today's turbulent times, find themselves increasingly distracted by external factors. Let's face it—we're all tempted to search the daily headlines for the signs of further decline or the glimmer of hope for an economic recovery. It is difficult to contemplate growth—let alone plan for it—when basic survival seems in question.

Rajesh Setty's latest book, *Upbeat*, sends a clear and compelling message to stay focused on what we can control and execute on a plan that is in tune with the changing marketplace. We must act to thrive, rather than just survive.

Upbeat brings together time-tested principles from the fields of biology, sociology, and psychology into a pragmatic guidebook for how to thrive at all times, but especially during this unprecedented economic downturn.

Drawing on his own experiences as a dot.com entrepreneur and a successful business leader and thinker, Rajesh begins by reminding us that our attitudes are a powerful tool for success. We can control our own negative talk and block out external sources that stop us from taking action.

I believe if we make it acceptable for our organizations to fail, they will. We need to expect our companies to outperform the competition in tough times and provide the tools—and the attitude—to make these results happen.

Even if we avoid the traps that can immobilize or derail us, we need the discipline, both mental and physical, to set and reach higher standards that will win over clients. Rajesh also reminds us that most humans function best as interconnected communities. We get help from our network by offering our own help. A solid network is about "give and take." Now is the time to take stock of your network. Finally, Rajesh focuses on the challenge of developing a plan for achieving solid business results that is relevant to the changing marketplace (what worked before doesn't necessarily work anymore). We must ruthlessly prioritize and take decisive action.

There will be winners and losers in the recession. *Upbeat* provides hope for leaders who don't want to watch from the sidelines. We must all be prepared to block out distractions, sharpen our focus, solidify our networks, and take advantage of the new opportunities. I recommend you spend a few hours experiencing the unique way Rajesh Setty weaves together pragmatic and even familiar insights into a new playbook for what is turning out to be a game that none of us have ever played in our careers!

RUSS FRADIN
Chairman and CEO, Hewitt Associates

Russ Fradin

MR. RUSS FRADIN is the chairman of the board and chief executive officer of Hewitt Associates, the world's largest provider of multi-service HR business process outsourcing (BPO), and the only firm fully integrating HR outsourcing and consulting. Mr. Fradin serves on the Board of Directors for both Gartner and The Executives' Club of Chicago, and is a member of The Illinois Business Roundtable.

He holds a master's degree in business administration from Harvard Business School and a bachelor of arts degree in economics from the University of Pennsylvania.

Acknowledging

I am really fortunate to have a loving family and a great set of friends, wonderful teachers and mentors in my life, and for the awesome people who are involved with me in one or more businesses. Without them, life would not be this meaningful. I thank them all from the bottom of my heart.

The first time I had an idea to write such a book was when I was building my first company in the middle of a recession. Not surprisingly, there was no time to write the book at that time. I also thought that it was too early to make a book out of issues in dealing with a recession, as I didn't know whether I would make it through the recession in the first place. But I did get through it – and in good shape. I want to thank everyone who helped us at the time.

A number of people (too many to list) in my personal network had a chance to review the early drafts for this book and provide their candid feedback. To all of them I just want to say, "I love you and thank you."

Of course, I have to thank Karthik Sundaram, my close friend and editor and designer of the book. A big thanks to

Karthik for making this book what it is today. Many thanks to Sunil Krishnan for designing the lovely cover. Shev Rush and Shelley Booze have been wonderful and they are helping me with PR and more for this and many other projects. Thanks to both of them.

I am deeply grateful to Mr. Russ Fradin, CEO of Hewitt Associates, who has kindly written the foreword.

My thanks also goes to David Wilk for taking care of a number of issues in getting this puppy out the door.

RAJESH SETTY

Contents

Why I wrote this book

The first company I founded in the U.S was in late 2000, right at the onset of a recession. At that time, it was caused by a dot-com bust or popularly called the "dot-bomb."

Looking back, I have to say that starting a company during that period was a blessing in disguise. It definitely did not feel like a blessing when I was going through it, though.

Nothing seemed to be working the way it should have worked. If I were to sum it up in one sentence, "everyone was trying to sell anything and everything to someone, and nobody was buying anything from anyone."

There were many reasons why I went wrong that I know today were wrong (give hindsight its due.) It was my first company and hence I had no track record to prove that I can make this work (irrespective of the times). The timing itself was wrong. The company's initial strategy was to provide a superior recruitment solution when nobody was hiring—in fact companies were firing employees almost everyday. There was no capital—except what the founders had invested. The business model was flawed. We could not have been in a worse shape.

In abundance was the passion and commitment to make it work. How to make this work was the million-dollar question. Since a recession was new to me, I did not spend too much time to understand it. We had so many "micro" problems to fix and not much time to look at the "macro" problems; although the "macro" problem was one of the big influencers of the "micro" problems that we were facing daily. I had read somewhere that a typical startup will change its business model thrice in the first eighteen months. When we had to change our business model, I did not hesitate because I thought we were simply falling into the category of a "typical" startup.

Not changing our model was not really an option, given the alternative was to simply shut the company down. So everyone around was VERY open to changing and morphing ourselves to be what the marketplace was wiling to place a value on.

Ego was not an issue nor did we have time for it.

The collective lack of "experience" engendered that everything happening around us was a "welcome" experience. One day we could make something out of this, I thought.

When things took longer than expected, I didn't know

whether it was because of the recession or because we didn't make the necessary changes on our end to make things work. There was no easy way to figure out one way or the other, and I picked the latter to be the cause since that provided me with a reason to have hope. That helped significantly as there was always something that we could change in every situation to achieve a result—better or different, who knew?

Cutting a long story short—it was more than two years before we were doing something that the marketplace was willing to pay a premium for. Things finally started going well after a LONG time.

But, I am not complaining, as the journey in itself was already a reward for all those that participated. Why was this a blessing, you may ask. Of the several reasons, I have picked five of them here:

- **Expanded Creativity**: We were forced to be creative in almost every aspect of the business. Constraints expand creativity and we had constraints like no other in the marketplace.

- **Cultivating Good Practices**: The practices that were put in place because of recession are applicable in "fair weather" times too. We were forced to adopt those practices but we were glad that we did.

- **Soaring Confidence**: Making it through the

recession with any success is tough. But if you do make it through your confidence soars. Any timeframe other than recession will have lesser constraints – so the logic is that if you can make it happen during times of recession, you have a better chance of making it happen when times are better.

- **Enhanced Mental Stamina**: The big lesson I learned was the importance of "staying power," to stick it out as long as it takes to make things happen. When I last checked, there was no course on how to improve your mental stamina but an exercise like this is an advanced course on this topic.

- **Professional and Personal Growth**: I doubt if I would have learned all the lessons that I was "forced" to learn about the marketplace, business and life in any other situation. What I was able to make of myself was well worth the price I paid for having built a business during a recession.

For those of you who are thinking about doing something and have been sitting on the sidelines, here is my $0.02—if you want to grow at a breathtaking speed and become someone that you will be proud of, the marketplace and the world has provided an opportunity again. Get off the wall, and jump in.

UPBEAT will help you quickly find the right rhythm to thrive in this great environment. UPBEAT talks about how to THRIVE during tough times. However, what is written here is NOT something that is applicable only during tough times—it should work well during good times too!

Stay Upbeat

Recession is here and everyone is invited to the party. Attendance is mandatory and you have just been given your free ticket.

Recession makes it hard for everyone. Rising unemployment, weak stock markets, tough credit markets, weak demand, fierce competition for that weak demand, uncertainty about when this will all end are just a start. It seems like there are just too many things out of our control during a recession. While this is generally true, there is one thing that is under our control—to have an UPBEAT attitude that's recession-proof.

How we survive through the recession and thrive will depend largely on what each of us did before we reached this place and what every one of us will do during these times.

There is no time-tested solution to make yourself recession-proof. Popular plans and prescriptions for recession won't work. That brings another question—if popular plans don't work, then where do we find the plans that do? There is no easy answer. If such a plan existed, it would NOT be affordable for most people, simply because it would be scarce.

So, what next? The solution, it seems, is that we have to "invent" our solutions to the recession problem. This would mean that we have to think and design a strategy based on several factors that include our strengths, our network, our risk appetite, our current savings, our health, and so on. This is news to most people—especially those who are used to working within large organizations where they are usually told what to do. You now have to think differently from the way you were thinking before whether you like it or not, There has to be a fundamental change inside you as there has been a fundamental change in the marketplace.

To think differently won't happen overnight but you have to start somewhere. My strong belief is that if you initiate change in the right direction, you will discover a solution for yourself very soon that outlasts any recession, and actually helps you thrive during such times.

Welcome to this journey and I thank you for giving me an opportunity to walk with you for the next few minutes. I am honored.

The Trap

There is a technical or official definition for a recession. It is a *period of general economic decline; specifically, a decline in GDP for two or more consecutive quarters*. Does it sound unconnected to your daily life? Sure, since it is not as significant as knowing how a recession manifests in your personal and professional life.

In your life, recession typically announces itself by showing you that what was working brilliantly before "suddenly" stops working.

Look around and you will see that you are not alone. It is showing up in lives of almost everyone around you. Things have stopped working "suddenly" and this phenomenon has become the talk of the town.

Soon, your daily conversations are frequently about what's not working in the marketplace, in the world and in your life.

The Daily Conversations

We live through our conversations, whether we give it the attention that they deserve or not. Susan Scott asks in her book *Fierce Conversations*, "Given that, while no single conversation is guaranteed to change the trajectory of a career, a company, a relationship or a life, any single conversation can—what is the conversation that has your name on it?"

Any single conversation has the potential to make a BIG difference in your life. With that in back of your mind, think about the conversations you have had TODAY. You will be shocked at what you learn.

For the last few days, most of my phone calls start with some variation of the following:

1. How is the market treating you?

2. What do you think about where the market is going?

3. The economy is VERY bad, don't know what else will occur…

Normally I get out of such a conversation in the first 60 seconds. Imagine having the same conversation with every caller during a day. Not only will I not learn anything new, I won't be able to get anything done in my life.

Engaging in conversations that will lead to nowhere continuously is a sure recipe for disaster. It is a "license for inaction." It is like saying "I don't want to do anything productive now. Give me a reason why I should." The current market conditions/economy/oil crisis/war will provide that reason, and it will be ample enough.

Watch your daily conversations. They may hold the key for how productive you are on a single day.

In the book "The Sun Also Rises," Hemingway paints a scenario where one of the key characters Mike Campbell is asked, "How did you go bankrupt?" and his response is "Gradually... then suddenly". This is so very applicable to a recession scenario. Actually, it is actually applicable to all of our lives—you don't fail suddenly; you fail gradually through a series of small failures everyday. The day you fail is just a culmination of all the small failures you have had.

You cannot afford to engage in "un-necessary" conversations everyday just because everyone else is doing it. Not everyone is going to the place that you plan and want to go; and if you want to survive and thrive, you should not be engaging in the same practices that people who have given up or resigned are roiling in. It is easy to get away with unproductive daily conversations because the cost of a single unproductive conversation may be very small. What is missed are:

1. Hidden costs for such conversations: You are thinking about these conversations long after the conversations are over
2. Collective cost: The sum total of the cost of these conversations over a period of time can be huge.

If our daily conversations are weak, we may end up starting a "sympathy exchange" movement.

The "Sympathy Exchange" movement

The "sympathy exchange" movement is in full swing. You may have already joined that movement or will be tempted to join it sooner than later. The criteria for joining this movement involves nothing more than actively giving and receiving sympathy during these tough times. There are no fees to be paid—just your precious time to actively participate and recruit others into the movement!

This movement is one of the fastest ways to bring down your productivity. So, whether you accidentally joined the movement or suddenly discover that you are part of it, you have to make plans to get out of it.

But how? The first step is to figure out the root cause of the problem—most probably a sense of being victimized. You feel you are a victim of circumstances (that are always beyond your control) and to validate your beliefs, your conversations tend to be around such circumstantial triggers. Surprise, surprise! Those you speak to are feeling the same way too. Secondly, I notice is that there are an awful lot of people who will worry about things that they don't have any control of. This is terrible. Everyone has enough things on which they have control on to worry about. If you are looking for sympathy, you are in luck. You will get plenty of it from a lot of the "victimized" others who are waiting to exchange sympathy.

In some sense, engaging in the "sympathy exchange" movement is like engaging in an argument. Both parties lose ultimately. If you agree that the "sympathy exchange" movement is an unproductive behavior, why in the world do we engage in such an act? The answer: Our Moods. Imagine trying to have a depressing conversation when you are in a great mood. You can't. Imagine having a fun conversation when you are in a depressing mood. You can't do that either.

Moods hold the key to shape the direction of your life.

I am in a Bad Mood

My teacher has been talking about moods for years. It took me a while to understand that I really CAN control my moods to my own benefit. Your moods are important not just because it will help people around you but because it will help YOU in the first place.

- Your moods will open or close opportunities.
- Your moods will help others assess whether to work with you or not.
- Your moods will influence your perspective of the world
- Your moods will determine how you view the marketplace
- Your moods will determine whether you will view something as an opportunity or a problem.

Simply said, your moods *will make it your day* or *make you resign*. And the best part about it is that you ARE in control of your moods. It's just that you might have forgotten that fact.

Well, you can change that right now, just as soon as you soon as you make a decision to change that. That's right now. However, to continue to be in the "right" moods throughout the rest of your life, you need discipline and commitment. But you really have to start somewhere and let that be today. Managing moods is a delicate act. Yes, you should not be in a bad mood but you should also not be in such an optimistic mood that you are out of touch with reality. One such "unrealistic" mood is to "want" something out of nothing: trying to take shortcuts to your destination.

Shortcuts will hurt you very quickly.

I need a shortcut!

The paradox in life is that shortcuts always take longer and/or cost more—thought it has not prevented people from trying them all the time.

It is tempting to take the easier path to reach somewhere sooner, especially when the times are tough. Recession is one of those times when any and all options to make something happen quicker will seem very interesting.

But recession is not an infinite that you are battling with finite time. Remember that your career spans over forty years. On the other hand, while nobody knows how long a recession will last, everyone knows that it has to end in a few years. Since your career will span much beyond the recession term, what you do during a recession will have a BIG impact on how your career and identity will evolve over a forty-year timeplan. So if you were thinking of doing something "quick-and-easy" to get by, stop and rethink! Quick-and-easy is never that, and if it were, everybody would be doing it to their benefit.

Your career and identity is built over your lifetime. Taking shortcuts to reach a good goal will only hurt your identity. Broken identities are hard to mend and it will take a long time to fix it (if you can ever fix it). In the Internet world we are living in, everything is recorded and is permanent.

Some shortcuts seem to work at first but will cause trouble later. One such shortcut is neglecting your health. Your body will only take care of you as much as you take care of it to take care of you.

Taking a shortcut in caring for your health will be expensive.

Health is the last thing on my mind!

You can't wish your problems away. "Health is wealth," is timeless wisdom. Recession or not, you are better off with good health than the alternative.

A recession provides a sort of "license" (only if you permit, of course) to start or continue unproductive or bad habits.

- You can explain away why you are not going to the gym or why you are not exercising—recession.
- Or why you are eating in those fast food joints everyday
- And why you are smoking or turning to alcohol again.

Most problems don't go away simply because you choose to ignore them – especially health problems. Health problems usually grow more complex until you can't ignore them anymore. If dealing with a recession is hard, imagine dealing with it when you are not in the best of health. You need to be in the best of your health to ensure that you are prepared to take on this challenge with full vigor. If you are not doing it already, this is the time to take on some healthy practices like exercising, walking, meditation, yoga—whatever you and your physician think will make you or keep you healthy.

The Discipline

I remember a quote by Jim Rohn, "Every disciplined effort has multiple rewards." This one advice has worked very well for me in my life. Not that I follow it all the time, but whenever I do, it has worked wonders.

Like any good idea, discipline is very easy to grasp as an idea but has no value unless it is implemented—and well. You have to get into the discipline of getting into the discipline, and get into the discipline of catching yourself when you get off the disciplined path.

As they say, every "overnight success" was the result of following a disciplined set of "good practices" over a period of time.

Once you have identified a set of positive practices, you need to make a commitment to yourself that you will be in this game for a LONG time.

In one word, be tenacious.

Tenacity is the name of the game

Giving up is easy. Anyone can do it. Only a few people can stick to something long enough—especially when things don't go the way they are supposed to go. As the old saying goes, when the going gets tough, the tough get going. Startups launched during recessions that have become successful have shown their ability to stick around long enough until they found something that clicked for them.

Every professional is like a startup during a recession—trying to do something new that has never been done before, because what has been done before has stopped working.

Recall any project that took you a long time to complete and your attitude and outlook when you were involved in that project. That same "can do" attitude and outlook is MANDATORY now. The difference is you probably have lesser resources now on your side while everybody around you is looking for a "short-term breakthrough."

On the positive side, the moment you cross a point in your quest to thrive, you will see less and less competition as most of the people gave up long before they reach anywhere close to where you are.

And soon enough, you will hunger to move on, everyday.

You need to be on a diet

A health diet, yes. More importantly, you have to be on a diet that is lean on unproductive behavior. Take an example of one such unproductive behavior—watching markets as they go up and down, over and over again. Unless you are a day trader, watching markets every other minute will be of no use.

Take this simple quiz. Replace company ABC with real companies that have been in the news last month. For every statement below, score 1 point if that news is DIRECTLY relevant to you and/or your business in the near future.

1. Company <ABC> is closing doors
2. Company A bought Company B in a fire-sale
3. The wild swing in the market is confusing investors
4. The government is discussing a new proposal for social security/Medicare/<pick your own problem that is not fixable>
5. The gas prices (or gold prices) are at a 12-month high/low

Now, forget the score. Did you observe that you were thinking HARD to find "relevance" of the news to your immediate future?

You are smart and you may be able to weld a connection between what's happening in the market to your business or personal life.

But don't try too hard to do that. Most media news can't affect you and/or your business. Such news finds space in the media because they are considered dramatic enough to gain readership. Media's got to have DRAMA. It is your duty to rise above the drama and focus on what's relevant for you.

This was an example of an unproductive practice but think about your own life and you can do an inventory of other unproductive practices that are plaguing your life. They may take up only few minutes a day or only a few hours a week but in the long run, they all add up and you will find your day produced very ineffective results.

Making the decision to get out of an unproductive behavior and to get into a productive behavior is easy. How do you ensure that you will keep this commitment?

The answer lies in personal accountability.

Be Accountable to Yourself

Recession time is hard on everyone, but this does not mean that you should get into a state of inertia, waiting for the times to pass. You need all your energy and more to make it through recession. When you need all four cylinders to fire on (and probably need to borrow two more) you can't try to win with half of them switched off.

From whom will the marketplace want to get help? Someone who is full of energy or a zombie?

The choice is clear. If so, how do you reform yourself?

There is always a way to get more out of who you are. If you were to give advice to yourself about how best to live your life, what would that advice contain? Let me help you here. That advice would ask you to stop some old practices, start some new practices and continue some existing practices. Even without anyone's help, you already know that you can make a few tweaks to your life to get more out of it.

Then, why wait?

Answers:

• You wait, because you can always provide some explanations and justify that it's really OK to be who you are.

- You wait, because there are no short-term implications for your bad behavior.
- You wait, because the long-term effects of lack of accountability are so far away that you don't have to worry about it now.
- You wait, because you can always blame others for your situation
- You wait, because you *can*.

I can go on. How you hold yourself accountable will define how you can turn upbeat.

And that calls for being flexible.

Stretch your flexibility and ADAPT

One day, you see that your microwave is gone and there is toaster in it is place. You can now complain that you don't fancy eating a sandwich or you can get used to eating one until the situation changes when you can get back your microwave oven.

You have to do something that you have never done before because a situation has been presented to you that has never been presented before—eat a sandwich or go hungry.

If you follow a routine that has produced a certain result, not changing it will not produce any different a result, simply because the world around you has changed. You can't change your practices overnight, so start today by making small changes. Your body and mind should get used to the change about making changes. You can start taking a big leap once you are comfortable with taking small steps. Once you are flexible, the next step is to "adapt" to the new order of the marketplace and the world.

Being flexible is to be open to change and to new ways of doing things. Adapting is to make new ways of doing things YOUR way of doing things. Once you adapt, you will not be conscious of the fact that you are changing, as the new methods and practices have become your methods and practices.

It is like changing to a new pair of shoes or new set of clothes as you grow up. You don't realize you are changing anything, and you just grow into wearing shoes of a different size. If you think about it, you will notice that wearing shoes of a smaller size is uncomfortable and it hurts.

I heard the "behind the scenes" story of an innovative marketing campaign "Will It Blend?" by a blender company called Blendtec. The campaign is simply a series of YouTube videos of the founder of the company (Tom Dixon) blending all sorts of things from marbles to iPhones. As of November 2008, these videos were watched 59 million times on YouTube and about 110 million times on the WillItBlend.com. There is now a DVD (for $10) offered on the website—a compilation of the first 50 of the "Will It Blend" videos.

George Wright, the brain behind this marketing campaign says that "the marketing department at Blendtec is a profit center – not a cost center".

Looking at the increase in sales—a spectacular 700%, Wright's flexibility and adaptability is paying off.

I had the good fortune of meeting with the serial entrepreneur Sam Wyly recently. Sam has been involved in building seven public companies that include Sterling Software, Bonanza Steakhouse, and Michaels Stores. When I asked for his advice to young entrepreneurs, Sam recommends that they practice persistence, be stubborn, stick with their ideas, and make them work.

If you are not doing these already, you will need to raise the bar for yourself.

Set higher standards

When asked why he is so successful, Michael Jordan reveals that his secret was to demand more from himself than anybody else ever will. Michael Jordan obviously sets higher standards for himself.

The marketplace sets no standards for mediocrity. Once higher standards are set, something reasonably below that will be considered as just mediocre. It is easy to get by being mediocre, and if you are lucky, you can do that for a long time.

The easiest way to get out of mediocrity is to set higher standards for yourself. You can do what is expected of you in a situation or you can do what is the best for the situation. We remember the gold, silver and bronze winners in an Olympic event, but not the person in the fourth place. The time difference may be very small but the person in the fourth place is rarely talked about. That's the difference between good and outstanding.

If you seek the benefits of gold medal winners, then be prepared to live up to their standards. Be prepared to put in the effort similar to what those winners do. Be prepared to work on your art and craft for a LONG time just like those gold medal winners do.

Take the marketplace standards for your craft as an input; and set them as baselevel standards for yourself. Now go ahead and simply raise the bars on them to set your own standards. The journey will really begin with the standards you set for yourself.

The Network

You can only do so much on your own. You need a network.

A network will amplify your capacity. You may ask, "By how much?" The answer really depends on how powerful your network is and how deep your relationships are. You may have added someone very powerful to your network but were acquainted with this person only since yesterday. This network may not work to your advantage today.

You may also have had someone that you have known for ages but the person is not powerful enough. This may not work either. Long-term relationships with powerful people provide you an unfair competitive advantage. Alright, stop right there now. Before you go off reaching out aggressively to those powerful people, remember that if you are not powerful yourself, there is no reason for those powerful people to be in your network. If what you give out is very small compared to what you get back, something is wrong, isn't it?

The easiest way to break free from this cycle is to offer to help make powerful people even more powerful. Provide them that extra boost to take them to the next level—wherever that is.

Give them help to help themselves.

They can do it. You can help!

(And, yes, you can do it. They can help too!) People need help a little bit of a push to get through these testing times. Right now, this minute, you should start focusing on helping people.

You may be thinking, "But wait a minute, I need a lot of help myself. Shouldn't I be going out and looking for help, rather than trying to help?" Agreed, but remember that everyone else in the marketplace is asking themselves the same question. If you are like everyone else, you will join a large majority, probably 90% of the crowd.

On the other hand, if you are in the minority crowd (the other 10%) where you have the capacity to help others, you will see a gigantic total addressable market (TAM). These are people in the majority 90% of the market. Premium will be paid to people who are there to offer help. You will also be creative if you are always thinking, "How can I help?" rather than thinking, "Why is this happening to me?"

My friend Raj Raheja at Heartwood Studios remembered an article in the *National Geographic* that discussed surviving in the wild. The author who had researched this topic found the most common factor that helped those who survived was their attitude: they set out to survive in their mind first before they actually survived. Tools and techniques help, but first, it all starts with your mind. When you develop an attitude to help others, you will lose focus on "worrying about things that you can't control" and you will be in an action mode: a good thing.

Now that you bought into the concept of building a network you find you are lost. Where do you begin?

This is where you bring your past back.

Yes, old is gold!

People are looking for good help from people whom they trust. So your trusted and long-standing relationships from the past are PURE gold.

Think about all of your old contacts from your professional. Now the next important step is to see how you can help them. NOT how they can help you.

You should really thank the times we are in. Finding old contacts today is easy through the Web. There are discussion groups, social networking sites, and alumni mailing lists to start with. Most importantly, you can email people who you know to begin a network, and through them, start connecting with people that you knew but had lost contact with.

All it requires is commitment and discipline to stick to a process and keep going at it until you are satisfied with the outcome. Always remember the golden rule. Give first!

If you forget to give, you become extra baggage in their lives.

Extra baggage costs more

You may not realize it but you may already be an "extra baggage" for someone out there. This happens often when you think that just because you know someone, you are entitled to make requests to that person.

Think about it. How long does it take to make a request? Typically not very long—all you have to do is ask in one or more of the following ways:

a. Call up someone and leave a voicemail

b. Call up someone, talk to them and make a request

c. Email someone

d. Send an instant messenger

e. Ask them when you meet them in person

Now, think about the time it takes for the other person to fulfill that request. Rarely can a request be fulfilled in the same time it takes to make it.

A creative request is one when fulfilling it is beneficial to the person who is being asked for it. A very good request is one you can design in such a way that the recipient of that request is thankful to you for making that request. In fact, he or she won't even feel that it was a request; they would think that it was an opportunity and they would be glad that you chose them to open up that opportunity for them.

You can avoid being a cost to others by THINKING before making any request. Time is in "short supply" for most people and people will like you for respecting this fact.

Actually, it does not require a lot of work to be an "extra baggage". You can create that feeling just by complaining.

Instead, why not be grateful?

Be Grateful

Yes, you are frustrated, things are not going well, and most of it is not your fault. However, do remember that in the grand scheme of things you are lucky enough to have the opportunity to think and do something about it. More than half the people in the planet don't have that opportunity. They have been living in recession-like conditions since their birth and probably live like that throughout their life.

You have been given the biggest gift of your life—your ability to THINK and do something about your current and future situations. Be grateful for that. Be grateful that you have come this far with whatever resources that you had under your disposal. Like I said, more than half the people in the world cannot even dream of the fraction of the resources that you have had until now.

Be grateful that if you do decide to change and make a difference in your life and in the lives of others, you can do it. More than half the people in the world can barely survive—so there is no question of making a difference in the lives of others for them.

Be grateful for all the gifts that others have given to you so far. It is easy to take people for granted and it is easy to feel entitled for what you have received. The world will look different if you start appreciating and feeling grateful for the little gifts that we all receive everyday.

Being grateful does not mean that you should be complacent. You can be in the "design and action" mode while being grateful.

Here is a simple trick that will trigger you to be grateful—rather than wanting what you don't have, start wanting what you already have. You will quickly realize that there are enough reasons for you to be grateful.

Focus on the right metrics

Many times I get a Facebook friend request to connect with somebody I know or who knows me, or doesn't know me. Two minutes later I get a LinkedIn request from the same person and a few more minutes later I get another request on another social network from the same person. It is almost like the person was in a hurry to update his score. Think about it:

- It is not just how many people you know.
- It is also just not who you know.

- It is "how" you know who you know.
- It is also how many people know you.
- It is also about how many people are glad that they know you.

If there is one metric that makes sense, it is the "extra capacity" you add in the life of another person in your network. With you being in their life, their life should be significantly better than without you being in their life.

Think about some of your close friends right now. Make a mental list of them. While you remember each friend, you also should remember their dream in life and their career.

Is this hard? Yes? Think again—should this be hard?

Focus on the right metrics. More importantly stop wasting your time on the wrong metrics. Again, how?

The Strategy

As they say, if you fail to plan, you plan to fail. Yes, there are always those rare people who become insanely successful without planning. There are anomalies everywhere. Unless "winning a lottery" is your game plan, you have no choice but to start designing and crafting your future. This becomes all the more important during times of recession.

The number one element that will give an input to any strategy is your honest assessment of the reality at hand.

Reality is real.

No strategy can ignore the facts. Reality will not change because of your strategy. It is your strategy that has to factor reality in. Ignoring reality won't help. It will catch up on you sooner than later.

If you don't have money to spend, you can't ignore it by swiping your credit card through a shopping spree. You can ignore the "no money" problem by using a credit card. But, one day, you will have to repay your credit card bills—with punishing interest!

If you are overweight, you don't solve the problem by changing your dress size. It will catch up with you sooner than later by reducing your energy level—or worse—with some health issue

If you are addicted to smoking, you don't try to solve the addiction problem by switching from a cigar to a cigarette. It will catch up with you sooner than later in the form of serious consequences to your body.

Imagination is a poor substitute for reality. Otherwise, people would imagine their way out of their troubles in real life. Reality is real. Now that you accepted reality, you will need a game plan to address this reality and accommodate it in your thrive plan.

This will call for a ruthless re-prioritization of your projects.

Re-prioritize ruthlessly

Do you have more things to do than hours in your life? That's the sad story in the lives of most people. During a recession, unfortunately the number of hours still remains the same, and the "things to do" will only go up.

A recession triggers an event (at least it should) that will force all of us to take a re-look at all our projects—both on the professional and personal front. Every project you started before the recession need not be completed. Some of those projects may have no meaning anymore. The beauty of shutting down non-important projects is that it provides you increased capacity to pursue the other (important) projects. So, there is no need to feel guilty that you are abandoning many projects. Where you need help—and you should aggressively pursue to get it—is in determining what projects to shelve and what projects to pursue.

One caveat: Your strategy should not move you away from solving your "core" problem or achieving your "core" objective.

Are you focusing on your "core" problem?

Here is a typical problem that I see day in and day out. You have a project. In your mind, you come up with a series of "possible" solutions to handle this project. Now when you want to explore how to implement these solutions, you will be creating new breakdowns that generate their own projects. One or more of the solutions becomes the source of new "project" at hand. You start solving the new project, which is OK but...when you go and ask for help, you have lost the focus on the "core" project. If this solution was wrong in the first place, no amount of help in solving the derivative problem will help you solve the core problem.

So you now start implementing your Plan B—your next best solution to the "core" problem. This will lead to new breakdowns and hence source of your new "problem." How do you get out of this vicious cycle?

The first step is to always remember your "core" problem or opportunity at all times. The second step is to explain the "core" problem or opportunity to the person from whom you are seeking advice/help. You can, of course, talk about what solutions you are thinking about to address the problem at hand but be completely "open" to hearing what the other person has to suggest. Once you ensure that you are always keeping the eye on the ball ("keeping the core problem/opportunity in focus") you have a better chance of getting the "right" help. A strategy is but a plan of action.

Whatever be your strategy, it has to be "highly relevant" to the marketplace.

Relevance please

It is often ironical that we are after what is out of our sight while blind to what is close to us. It happens in life and it happens in our business.

We try to pursue skills just because everyone else is. In that rush, we forget to capitalize on the skills that we already have.

You can change that.

Once you identify assets in you that are relevant in the changed marketplace, begin sharpening them aggressively. If there are other assets that you wish you had, try and see if you can find partners with those assets who can complement you.

In other words, grow your assets but take care of your weaknesses through creative partnerships: because you don't have the time to go and try to fill the gaps NOW.

Whatever you do, your strategy must be flexible to accommodate changing marketplaces.

You have to be open to exploring and creating new offers in the changed marketplace.

New markets, here we come!

The million-dollar question is, "Should you focus on the existing market or innovate and try to explore new markets?"

My take is that you can start making mini-exceptions during a recession. New opportunities open up because of fresh breakdowns that occur during this period. Since so many people are watching for these gaps that create new opportunities, you have a small time window to capture them for your advantage. Keep an open eye and open mind to explore new markets. That might very well be the "turning point" that you are looking for yourself and your company.

Yes, the resources are less and you need to focus all your energy on whatever else you are doing. However, you also need to be alert that you are not driving towards a cliff blindly.

While focus is very important, rules and structures change during a recession. Focusing on something that's not working anymore will not lead to a miracle. You must cultivate the attitude of flexibility while you retain focus.

The Action

Ideas are more meaningful when they are implemented. One of your most compelling offers in the marketplace should help someone implement their ideas—help them take their ideas from concept to reality.

In a recession, there will be an oversupply of people who may be offering the same kind of help that you may be offering. If you have to rise above the noise to be heard, you have to start first by telling better stories than others in the marketplace.

Why? Because, others will stop to hear the unique story you are telling.

We are hooked to stories from a very young age. We liked them as young kids, and have not stopped liking them as we grew up. We CRAVE for good stories. If your story won't cut it in the marketplace, chances are you will have a tough competition from someone else whose story is better than yours—or can at least tell his or hers better than you do.

How do you learn to tell a better story? First, it starts with your commitment to want to learn to tell a better story. It has to be in your background all the time, so you start noticing good stories rather than just being gripped by them. Once you start noticing them, you can get expert help to de-construct some of the best stories that are being told. This is where mentors and teachers come in. They can help you get to the bottom of the story and probably answer the following questions:

- What was the most compelling piece of the story?
- How was it designed, crafted and delivered?
- What made the story credible?
- If somebody else had told the same story, would it have had the same impact?

Once you have de-constructed a story, try to model your story from what you learnt, and see how compelling you can make it. Try it out and see if you are succeeding. If not, you can go back to drawing board and re-craft the story. If not, get help from someone who can tell your story better. If you don't get this right, you will be part of the noise. If your story is a hit, you are still not there yet as people want to know "who" is telling the story.

This is where your history of accomplishments from the past will come in handy to demonstrate clear thought leadership on a topic.

Demonstrate Clear Thought Leadership

In these market conditions, nobody would want to hire someone who has

a. No help to offer and

b. Worried about their own survival

If you don't have any help to offer in these times, then worrying about it won't help. People want to work with people who have help to offer.

So, now if you do have help to offer but you are not visible, you will lose out to people who have help and are also visible in the marketplace.

The fastest way (but one that would have taken a long time of your past) to become visible is to demonstrate clear thought leadership in the areas where you can offer the most help. This requires you to be in action.

During times of recession, you have to accelerate any and all of your projects that will CLEARLY demonstrate your thought leadership in the marketplace. Of course, if you are busy victimizing yourself, you won't have time to do that.

Remember, "Proof of accomplishment" creates an assessment of clear thought leadership in the minds of others—

facts to prove that you are an authority on that topic.

Recession or no recession, people are looking for "good" help. They are talking about their needs, wishes, wants and concerns somewhere and that "somewhere" is precisely where you have to be with a clear demonstration of your thought leadership.

Mediocrity is everywhere and people who are competing at this level will face the fiercest competition. Providing discounts won't help either as it will make a mess of the market, and even harder for mediocre people. Thought leaders and real experts will be at a premium (rightly so).

Again, you may quickly realize that you don't have all the power to execute this on your own.

You need to get "good" help quickly.

You better get "better" help!

You are insufficient on your own. I am insufficient on my own.

From the time you and I get up from our beds, we are dependent on a bunch of people in the world to coordinate actions with us to help us get through our days.

If you don't believe it, try this thought experiment: Imagine all the traffic lights on your way to work go bonkers and stop working. Think how it would be to drive to work in this condition. You will need to coordinate with six other lane drivers across three different visual angles, and agree to move in a synchronized manner, assuming all of them are as careful and good a driver as you are (and assuming you are one).

In a recession, more than ever, it pays to work with good people, if not with the best. The market condition is like the traffic signal where the lights are not working. You will need to coordinate with others, give and get help to move forward.

So what do you do?

Get the best help your money can afford. You can view this as an expense or an investment OR as a premium you pay for a "Recession Insurance Policy." We know that:

- Our actions largely determine where we are going
- Our thoughts precede our actions
- Our attitude shapes our thoughts
- Our awareness influences our attitude
- Our knowledge raises our awareness
- Our teachers amplify our knowledge

So this is the time (if you are not already doing it) to aggressively pursue finding and seducing the "right" teachers to help you survive and thrive in this recession. Actually, you have to rush on this one.

Why? Simply because there are not many people who can offer you that help and they have limited capacity to do so. Even if you can afford them and they want to work with you, they probably won't have the time to do it.

Two things to note: First, "good" help is scarce—otherwise everyone will have access to it and it won't be a competitive advantage anymore. Second, "good" help is expensive because it is "scarce." So where do you find the money to afford "good" help?

The answer is to spend less on things that will add less value so that you can spend MORE on "good" help.

Spend less AND spend more

Spending less is easy to understand, albeit tough to follow. You have to cut down on all your expenses—anything and everything that won't add "enough" value. Think about the number of trips to your favorite coffee shop; or those visits to the cinemas, when you could rent from your local library. Yes, this would mean changing habits. You can do it by choice or you can wait for situation to force it upon you. It is better that you do this by your choice.

Spending more is difficult to understand. This is your time to increase your investments in yourself:

- To be the best at who you are
- To be someone who will stand out from the crowd
- To be someone who has a powerful personal brand
- To be someone that demonstrates thought leadership
- To be someone who has powerful relationships
- To be someone who can credibly add "value" to the marketplace
- To be someone who can get things "done"

This requires hard work, commitment, and most importantly, the willingness to make necessary investments to get there. You are the biggest asset that you have. If that's true, why not make the necessary investments to grow that asset, whatever the situation in the marketplace? Lastly, being prepared to play the game is not the same as playing the game.

You need to play the game to get somewhere.

Ring-side seats are safe, but...

I remember Teddy Roosevelt's famous quote:

> *"It is not the critic who counts; not the man who points out how the strong man stumbles, or where the doer of deeds could have done better. The credit belongs to the man who is actually in the arena, whose face is marred by dust and sweat and blood; who strives valiantly; who errs, and comes short again and again, because there is no effort without error and short coming; but who does actually strive to do the deeds; who spends himself in a worthy cause; who at the best knows in the end the triumph of high achievement, and who at the worse, if he fails, at least fails while daring greatly, so that his place shall never be with those cold and timid souls who know neither victory nor defeat."*

Summarizing it one word, "Play!"

Running with the ball is an exercise fraught with risks. You are at the risk of not playing right, playing too early, playing a tad late, closing your eyes at the wrong moment and missing the ball completely or simply getting hurt. There is a lot at stake while playing. On the other hand, you can take a ring-side seat and watch the game unfold. You are not on the ground but you are VERY close—you are almost on the ground playing.

You can comment about how the player should have swung a bit early, a bit late, at slightly a different angle, with slightly a different speed. It won't take long for you to make a dozen recommendations to "fix" the way the player should have played to win.

It's a lot of fun to do that, but, make no mistake. The experience on the ring-side seat is NEVER going to be the same as the experience of going out there and playing.

Think about it. Who do people want to follow: someone who is on the field playing or someone sitting on the ring-side seat and commenting on how to play?

Play!

A Final Note

You have heard this before: a problem and an opportunity are like the two sides of a coin. Depending on what side you are looking, you will take different actions.

Recession provides an unprecedented opportunity for you to lead and make something happen. Recession begs for fresh leadership.

Why?

Recession leaves a large majority of people shaken and stirred (yes, I am a James Bond fan) because what is familiar to them and what has been working all along will stop working.

The initial reaction from people will be to continue to hang on to something that they have known and be familiar with all along. People will quickly realize that what they are hanging on to may not take them to a safe location; in fact, it becomes clear that continuing to hang on will hurt them more than it will help them. This creates a void. A BIG void! Or we can say this creates an opportunity. A BIG opportunity! People are looking for direction and help. The more you have to offer, more opportunities open up and more people are willing to let you lead. So, what are you waiting for? Isn't it time to be upbeat about this recession?

Thrive!

About Rajesh Setty

RAJESH SETTY lives in the Silicon Valley with his wife Kavitha and son Sumukh. He is intimately involved in working with like-minded entrepreneurs to bring good ideas to life, and spread their adoption. He frequently holds interactive workshops and delivers speaking sessions in growing human wealth.

Website: www.rajeshsetty.com
Blog: www.lifebeyondcode.com
Twitter: www.twitter.com/UpbeatNow

Upbeat D-I-Y Helpbook

They say that the best helping hand you have is at the end of your arm. You have more power than you can imagine helping yourself. The goal of this companion DIY Book is to provide you a kick start to put a few ideas from the book into action.

This means work, I know. I also know there is no other easy choice. Plans are important and useful. But, execution is where we all get stuck. This companion book provides some starter ideas for each section but they are not complete by any means. I am sure you can come up with your own ideas too.

Let your creative juices start flowing. Pick one or two sections that intrigued you and pen down your own ideas of how you are going to implement what you have learned.

All the best!

RAJESH SETTY

The Trap | The Daily Conversations

Your daily conversations have a way bigger impact than you can imagine. What you choose to say and what you choose not to say have equal impact. Who you are spending time with and who you are not spending time with will have an impact. You can change that for the better if you choose to. Here are some ideas:

1. Marshall Sylver talks about using the right vocabulary in his book "Passion, Profits and Power." Your choice of words in the daily conversations is extremely important. Marshall talks about the use of word "But." When somebody says, "We can do this BUT the economy is bad," remember all they are saying is that they can't do something, because the economy is bad. Try using "And" instead of "But" and suddenly the situation looks more positive. The reframed version will be - "We can do this AND the economy is bad." Doesn't sound too bad, eh?

2. Set "hard stops" for meetings. When both of you know that you have only a limited time for "that" meeting, you will be forced to get on with the real business soon.

3. Choose people who will lift you up rather than bring you down. Make an attempt to spend more time with them this week. You cannot eliminate "dissipaters" (those who drain

your energy) from your life but if you reduce the time you spend with them, you can use that extra time to spend with energizers (those who amplify your energy)

The Trap | The "Sympathy Exchange" Movement

You can get sympathy for almost nothing – just pretend to be a victim. Note that you don't have to be a victim; you only need to pretend to be one. In return, sympathize with the other person who might also be pretending to be a victim. Ultimately both of you may get nothing out of this "sympathy exchange" program. Here are some things you can do to get out of this program:

1. When someone close to you is looking for sympathy, you will do them more harm than help if you give it to them. Stop for a moment and give them hope or inspiration.

2. Invest in one or more inspirational books. Read a few minutes at the start of your day. Read anything that will lift your spirits up. If you are in a good mood, it is hard to start or continue a depressing conversation.

3. While giving sympathy for no reason is bad, looking for sympathy for no reason is worse. Donate a dollar every time you go looking out for sympathy from someone else.

The Trap | I am in a Bad Mood

Moods are probably heavily under-rated. How you do what you do depends first on your mood and then on other things like capacity and competence. The willingness to do something well is first influenced by your mood. Here are a few things to consider:

1. What is your mood right now? Imagine someone is asking this question every now and then during the day. If you are conscious about your moods, you won't be sucked into living in bad moods Learn to observe your moods. Once you notice them, you will soon start fixing them.

2. Laugh often. Have a joke book handy if you need a reason to laugh.

3. Look for help everywhere that will provide help in lifting your mood. There is enough help out there.

For example, a simple search on the internet got me this wonderful this tip on moods from Cheryl Rainfield – "Your sense of smell is a quick and easy route into your emotions, and is one of the most powerful ways to evoke memory. Smell something from a time when you felt happy or joyful or loved that reminds you of someone you love, or that just makes you feel good. Pure citrus scents (natural, not fake) are naturally uplifting. Many people are also drawn to the scents of cinnamon; vanilla or benzoin; favorite perfumes or colognes; the scent of cookies being baked or a favorite meal; etc."You can get more information at http://www.cherylrainfield.com/

The Trap | I Need a Shortcut

Unfortunately there are no shortcuts in life. Look at nature (examples: a tree growing out of a seed, a baby from conception to birth) and you will see that it takes time for things to happen. Here are some ideas to get out of the shortcut trap.

1. Read the memoir of someone accomplished that you love and respect. You will notice that if there was ever an "overnight success," years of hard work was put in before realizing that "overnight success."

2. Resurrect a long-term project that you abandoned. Make sure that the project is relevant for today. What is golden is getting into the habit of completing projects – small or big.

3. Look beyond yourself. Who among your loved ones are trying to take a shortcut? When will you have a conversation with them about the right way of doing things?

The Trap | Health is the Last Thing on My Mind

Health can be ignored until it can't be ignored any more. Bad habits when it relates to health show up as consequences only in the long-term. So it becomes easy to get into these habits unless you are disciplined enough. Sadly, it does not take a lot of effort to take care of your health — you have to put some good practices that you religiously follow DAILY. Here are some ideas:

1. Schedule a "walking" meeting rather than a sit-down meeting. It may seem uncomfortable at first because you are used to a meeting with your notebook and at a table. However, you will get used to it very soon. Sometimes not having notes or presentation slides can have its own advantage.

2. A common excuse I hear from people is that they haven't found the time to go to the gym. If you think about it, there are healthy people in the world who have not even heard of a

gym. To get into an exercise routine, a gym helps but it is not mandatory to go to a gym. For instance, you can practice yoga and all it requires is a yoga mat—and a good dose of dedication. Think about your resources and time required to exercise. You may be fooling yourself with those excuses.

3. Take the stairs rather than the elevator when possible.

The Discipline | Tenacity is the Name of the Game

Long-term thinking is generally hard as there is nothing substantial to gain in the short-term. The world around you demands results in the short-term. It doesn't care about your long-term goals or objectives. There is only one person who has the responsibility to care and it is YOU. If you give up, nobody else can help. The will power to stay in the game for the long-haul is a skill and you need to work on honing it. Here are some ideas:

1. Categorize your projects and identify the percentage of projects that you are working on that are "long-term." Is this a healthy percentage? If not, you can work towards changing that mix right now. Pure short-term thinking will hurt big time in

the long run.

2. What assets are you building that will pay back in the long term? If there are no assets that you are developing, it will only be "YOU" that will have to work for you. There will be absolutely no leverage and this will hurt you.

3. As they say, what is important is not whether you fall or not but how fast you bounce back when you fall. The biggest risk is to not to take any risk at all. In the long run, you will fall, get up and fall again. The question is, are you ready to get into this roller-coaster ride for a LONG time?

The Discipline | You need to be on a diet

I have worked as a journalist before (that was my very first job) and there has to be "drama" in the news — otherwise it's not newsworthy. In your busy life, you may not have the time to separate the "drama" from the "facts". Worse yet, you might be gripped by the "drama" part of the news more than the "news" part of the news. That hurts. Here are some ideas:

1. Stop watching the nightly news for a week. You will

notice that you didn't miss much and you can catch up on everything in a fraction of the time on the Internet.

2. Turn off the radio during your commute. Listen to a good audio book instead.

3. Request your friends and family to help you with your "news diet" for a week. Ask them not to bring up any news that is not VERY relevant to you or your business for a week. One week of "no drama" won't hurt you in anyway.

The Discipline | Be Accountable to Yourself

Keeping a promise that you made to yourself can be VERY hard. Why? Simply because there is no punishment ever for not fulfilling that promise. You can always come up with an explanation and cite external sources for the reason for not keeping that promise. If it becomes a habit, very soon you can't get anything done. Here are a few ideas to consider:

1. Stop for a second before you make the next promise. Think carefully whether you have the necessary resources to fulfill that promise. If yes, go ahead and if not, it is better to not

promise than to not deliver.

2. Make a small commitment to yourself – something that you know you can be VERY sure of sticking to it. Then stick to it. You get a bump in your self-esteem. Repeat it with a slightly larger commitment. Keep doing this until you make a life-changing commitment.

3. If you have trouble being accountable to yourself and/or good at creating "extremely compelling" excuses for why something was not done, try getting help. Ask a close friend to hold you accountable.

The Discipline | Stretch your flexibility and ADAPT

Really, it's not like you have a choice on the topic of flexibility. As the world changes, your offers have to change. Here are some starter ideas:

1. Start driving to your office on a different route every day of the week, however uncomfortable it is to you. You need to get used to doing things differently.

2. Read a book on a topic that is outside of your normal

reading habit. Start an activity that will activate some right-brain thinking – art, craft, and so on.

3. Watch a foreign language movie and discuss it with a friend.

The Discipline | Set higher standards

The marketplace sets standards for assessing your performance out there. But the marketplace won't prevent you from setting standards higher than what the marketplace has set for you. Here are some starter ideas.

1. What are people close to you expecting out of you? What are you expecting out of yourself? Is what you are expecting out of yourself WAY higher than what others are expecting out of you? If not, why not?

2. Expectation, if used right, is a great motivator. What are your expectations of yourself for your life and your career? Remember that you are now leading a life based on your "implicit" expectations. You are making choices based on those "implicit" expectations. This will work as long as everything is pretty in the marketplace. In the long-run, it is a strategy bound to fail.

3. I was fortunate to have worked for bosses who expected a LOT out of me. Are you working for someone who expects a LOT out of you? If not, what are you waiting for?

The Network | They can do it, you can help!

Building a network is important and has big paybacks. But that comes later. Your first job is to "give" significant help to the network that you are trying to build.

1. List your top 25 friends. List their dreams against each one of them. If you know their dreams, fill in "1" there. Now total up to create your "friend-dream-score." May be you can do something to drive the score higher in the next few weeks?

2. Right now stop reading this and do something that will make their day for someone in your network.

3. How many calls for help/support have you received from your friends in the last one week? If none, there is something wrong. Either it means that people don't need help (which is not true) or it means that they don't think you can help (which is bad).

The Network | Yes, Old is Gold

The good part is that you have a history and I have a history. We all have histories. It is just that some people capitalize on their histories while most of them will write-off the past. The best place to start building your network is to look at your past. Here are some starter ideas.

1. Are you actively involved in your Alumni Networks (school, college and past companies)? If yes, what are you contributing to that network? If no, when are you going to start?

2. Who among your friends from the past would you wish to be in close contact with? What will you do this week to get in touch with that person?

3. Do you know where your past colleagues are working today? Who among those past colleagues can you reach out in the next few weeks and what will be your offer to help them with their current projects?

The Network | Extra baggage costs more

You don't want to have extra baggage in your life. Others don't want that too. Whatever you do, try to avoid being an extra-baggage in other's lives. Please note that the ideas outlined here are for your business relations and not for your personal relationships. So, here are those starter ideas:

1. Look at your next email. Just before hitting the "Send" button, think carefully – what is in this for the recipient? They have to make an investment to read it. But is the return on that investment clear? Are you confident that they will get something out of making that investment? If not, what can you do to fix it?

2. Look at your next meeting request. Before you ask someone to take time out to meet with you, do the same ROI calculations for the other person. Everyone is busy and has limited time. Meeting with you means that they can't meet with anyone else at the SAME time. It's an opportunity cost for them if this meeting does not add ENOUGH value to them.

3. Stop before you dial that next number. This phone call is important for you but is it equally or more important to the person that you are calling? If not, what can you do to make it so?

The Network | Be Grateful

There is absolutely no way you can survive and thrive on your own – which means that LOTS of people are helping you to make it happen. The question is, are you "thanking" all of them enough? A few ideas to consider:

1. Who did you thank today? Email, call or send a thank you note. Do what you are comfortable with – but please do that today.

2. Who are you going to thank tomorrow?

3. Buy a hundred "Thank You" cards and always keep them next to your desk. If you have not exhausted them by the end of twelve months, something is seriously wrong.

The Network | Focus on the Right Metrics

Social Media has changed people's perceptions about what it really means to be "connected." The real metrics are not the number of connections on LinkedIn or the number of friends on Facebook or Myspace. If you think of your network as a lifetime investment rather than a short-term phenomenon, you will look at the whole issue differently. To shift your thinking, here are some questions:

1. How many people in your network feel blessed that you are in their network?

2. How many people in your network feel that they have more capacity than before because you are in their network?

3. How many people in your network see more possibilities in their life because you are in their network?

The Strategy | Reality is Real

Unfortunately imagination is a poor substitute for reality.

1. How are you getting your facts today? Are the sources trust-worthy? If they are not, what are you going to do to change that? If the local newspaper is the only source of your information, you are in trouble. The world has moved on.

2. How are you keeping abreast of the trends that WILL affect your industry, job, company and your country? Sometimes people say that we shouldn't care about it too much as "whatever happens to everyone else will happen to them too." When you

are one of the people who are affected by something, it gets too personal and it may be very late.

3. Reality is real. True. However, it is also an interpretation by someone. Otherwise, how will you make sense of something new – something that you have not heard of every before? If this is the case, it becomes very important to know who the people are whose interpretations you are listening to. What are their accomplishments and why are you listening to them?

The Strategy | Re-prioritize Ruthlessly

You notice a change in the marketplace when valuations fluctuate. The best response is to change so that you continue to be relevant and valuable to the marketplace.

1. Do an inventory of your business and personal projects. What projects are you working on and how will each of them help you with your long-term objectives?

2. What happens if you abandon one of your current projects? What are the stakes?

3. What happens if you succeed beyond your imagination on

your current project? Will you be happy with what you would have got out of the success of the current project? Alternatively, what other project could you have engaged to get better results than what you might be getting?

The Strategy | Are you focusing on the core problem?

We are always working on one or more projects. Typically these projects are sub-projects of one or two big projects. When you get deeply engaged in a sub-project and it gets complex, you lose track of the fact that this was part of a big project.

1. Look at your current project. This is typically a sub-project of a bigger project. What is the bigger project? Understanding this for every project will force you to look at the big picture.

2. How do you know you are focusing on the core problem or opportunity? What questions are you asking yourself to determine that you have got this covered? What other question could you be asking to make this bullet-proof?

3. Lastly, what is the BIG project you are working on now?

Do you have the right kind of structure to execute this project? How much of your personal time are you spending on this BIG project today? Are you happy about it? If not, what are you doing to change it?

The Strategy | Be Relevant

Relevance is on the top of everything. Whatever you bring to the marketplace has to be relevant. Just being relevant won't get you a premium but not being relevant will ensure that your offers are commoditized and pushed to the bottom of the chart. Here are some questions to ponder about:

1. How relevant are you and/or your company to the marketplace?

2. How relevant is your current project to the marketplace?

3. Continuing on the path you are on, how relevant will you be to the marketplace five years from now?

The Strategy | New markets, here we come.

Every discontinuity presents new opportunities. When gas prices become super-expensive, air travel may suffer but traveling on land will increase. What is a problem for airlines is an opportunity for someone else. This is also a time for several old markets to disappear and other new markets to appear. Your strategy has to be flexible to make the most of these new markets. In fact, there has to be a conscious effort to be on the lookout for virgin markets. Here are some ideas:

1. "Knowledge arbitrage" is exploring how something that works very well in an industry or domain be applied to another industry or domain. Think and be open to applying knowledge from other industries or verticals into your own industry or vertical. Customize and "borrow," while being transparent.

2. Next, look at the value chain. The key questions to answer are – "What happens before you engage with a customer or after you stop your engagement with a customer?" Once you identify the answers for the two questions, see how your offering can be extended to encroach into one of the areas (before or after) to extend your value chain.

3. Lastly, look at creative partnerships. Who can you

partner with creatively to enter another industry or domain? What is something unique that you can bring to this partner so that he or she is motivated to engage with you?

The Action | All others can hear is the story you are telling them

Stories make it easy to communicate something. There is a story always going on and all others can hear is the story you are telling them. Some things to think about:

1. Watch the movie Titanic. It's about a ship that sinks. Almost everyone who watches the movie already knew that the ship sinks, yet the movie grips everyone for three hours. That's storytelling. Can you tell the story about your business or work in the same fashion?

2. Craft a story about your work and tell this to a friend. Is he or she excited about this? If yes, ask him or her what part excited them most? If not, go back to the drawing board.

3. A mini saga is a story told in exactly 50 words. Not 49 or 51 but exactly 50. Write a mini saga. Whatever it is that you will write about – one thing you will notice is that you will

gain more clarity on that topic. You can see a few examples at http://www.squidoo.com/minisaga

The Action | Demonstrate clear thought leadership

When the going gets tough, people look for help from the "real" experts— those that demonstrate clear thought leadership. Being a thought leader is something that you can't just wish. It's not something that you announce to the world – it's an assessment that others make of you. Some questions to ponder about:

1. How do your past clients/employers/bosses remember you? Is that powerful enough?

2. How do you want your future network to remember you?

3. What actions have you taken to ensure that your world knows what you bring to the marketplace?

The Action | You better get "better" help.

If everything is equal between two competitors, one that has "access" to better help will always win. If you want a clear competitive advantage, setup structures so that you have "access" to better help than your peers. Some places to start:

1. Do you have one or more mentors? If not, what are you waiting for?

2. Is the "right" team working on your current project? If not, what is your plan for getting the "right" help to get this project moving in the right direction?

3. Are you willing to pay the "right" price to get the "right" help? Remember, you pay the price or you pay the price for not paying the price.

The Action | Spend less AND spend more

Cutting costs indiscriminately is a knee-jerk reaction to your problems. Some of these costs may be long-term investments.

The focus has to be to continue spending on "investments" and continue cutting on "non-critical expenses." Here are some questions to start with:

1. What expenses can you knock off starting tomorrow?

2. With the money saved, what new investments can you make in yourself?

3. Even if you can't cut any expenses, what new investments should you make in yourself today so that you are prepared for tomorrow?

The Action | Ring-side seats are safe, but...

Vance Havner said it beautifully: "It is not enough to stare up the steps – we must step up the stairs." Planning is a necessary but not a sufficient condition. Plans are worthless without execution. Unless your job is "planning," the world does not reward you for "what you are going to do" – it waits for you to act and make things happen. The majority of people have plans, only a small set of them act. You want to be in that small set of those people who do act. It has to start somewhere. Some ideas:

1. What was your most recent failure? If you are thinking too much about it, you may be sitting on the sidelines for long. It is time to roll-up your sleeves and get into action.

2. What is a long-term project that you have been thinking about for a LONG time but have not done anything about? Rather than jumping into action, please think and list ALL the reasons (excuses) for not taking action. Variants of these reasons or excuses are what will stop you from taking action in similar projects. May be you have to think about these "stumbling blocks" that are hurting you.

3. Lastly, what is the ONE action that you will take as a result of reading this book? How will you hold yourself accountable for doing that?

Bulk Purchases of
Upbeat:

Bulk purchases and customized editions of this book are available to purchasers at favorable rates. Additionally, content in this book may be used by arrangement with the publisher for training and other purposes. Please contact the publisher for further information:

Special Sales Manager
Ashoka Books
Creative Management Partners LLC
8 Gray's Farm Road
Weston CT 06883
(203) 454-4454
david@booktrix.com

Author Engagement

RAJESH SETTY works with start-ups, mid-size companies and divisions within large corporations in idea-workshops, talent-growing engagements, and interactive coaching sessions.

For engaging with him, please visit:
http://www.rajeshsetty.com/about/speaking

You can follow him on his blog at
http://www.lifebeyondcode.com

or on Twitter at
http://www.twitter.com/UpbeatNow

Forthcoming Titles:

People rely on blogs to get information, to make decisions, and to keep up-to-date with what is happening. Blogs increasingly create a powerful impact on our lives. BLOGTASTIC! will help bloggers create significant audience advantages through precise tools and technics. Watch out for the title in the Fall of 2009.

Notes

_____

_____

_____

_____

_____

_____

_____

_____

_____

_____